DICTION
ANIMALS

Malcolm Higgins

Contents

Rigby

A Harcourt Achieve Imprint

www.Rigby.com
1-800-531-5015

Amphibians

Amphibians are animals with smooth, wet skin. They have cold blood. Amphibians live in water when they are young. Most amphibians live on land when they get older.

salamander

frog

newt

Birds

Birds have two wings and two feet.
They have warm blood.
They have feathers, too.
Most birds can fly, but some
birds can't.
Instead of flying, they move
by running or swimming.

eagle

robin

penguin

Fish

Fish live in water.

They have cold blood.

They have gills that help them breathe under water.

Fish have smooth scales all over their bodies.

goldfish

eel

shark

Invertebrates

Invertebrates are animals without backbones.
They don't have any bones at all.
Many invertebrates have hard outsides.
This helps keep their soft insides safe.

spider

beetle

lobster

Mammals

Most mammals have hair
or fur on their bodies.
They have warm blood.
Almost all mammals live on land,
but some live in the water.
Even mammals that live in water
must come up to breathe air.
All mammals feed their babies
with milk.

dolphin

dog

humans

Reptiles

Most reptiles are covered with rough, dry scales.
They have cold blood.
Most reptiles live on land, but some live in water.
Reptiles that live in water must come to the top when they need air to breathe.

snake

alligator

turtle

Vertebrates

Vertebrates are animals
with backbones.
They have other bones
inside their bodies, too.
Bones help the animals
keep their shapes.
Amphibians, birds, fish,
mammals, and reptiles are
all vertebrates.

goldfish

wren

toad

snake

horse

Index